ENDORSEMENTS

"Before a personal relationship with Christ, baseball was [Rob's] life. After he surrendered his life to Christ, baseball became an instrument to share the unmeasurable love and grace of Christ. It has been a great honor knowing Rob since 1997, and seeing the Lord use him and his family in His mighty way."

—**Duffy Guyton, Chief Development Officer at Mid-America Baptist Theological Seminary, Cordova, TN; pastor of Shelby Forest Baptist Church, Millington, TN; and former pitcher with the St. Louis Cardinals**

"*The Reliever: My Journey from Pitcher to Preacher* is a cautionary and inspiring story that kids and adults will enjoy reading. It was a thrill, as his high-school teammate, to catch Rob's fastball. But it does not compare to the excitement of learning about Rob's journey to his new life as a preacher."

—**Dave Barr, former quarterback, University of California at Berkeley and the St. Louis Rams, Sacramento, CA**

"Rob's story is powerful! A great collection of baseball stories and a testimony of God's power at work in the middle of a baseball diamond."

—**Nolan Porter, pastor, Salem Avenue Baptist Church, Rolla, MO; and pitcher at Sul Ross State University 2004–2006**

"In *The Reliever*, Rob shares his life story from his greatest victories to his greatest defeats. Everyone, especially athletes, needs to read this book. The Reliever will change your life!"

—**Scott Carter, high-school basketball coach and evangelist, Hatley, MS**

"As you read this book, you will discover authenticity."

—Dr. David Tolliver, chaplain and pastor, Jefferson City, MO

"*The Reliever* reveals how Rob overcame the disappointment of his shattered dream and found fulfillment by turning his life over to Jesus Christ."

—Dr. Bobby Mullins, executive director, Back to the Basics Ministries; and A Fresh Start TV program pastor, Fellowship Baptist Church, Hernando, MS

"My grandson Bo said he was going to play professional baseball. I want him to read this book! I believe that *The Reliever* will help him realize that putting God first is the way to begin his baseball career."

—Al Ziegler, businessman, Greenville, MS

"This book [is] very touching, inspiring, and really heartwarming."

—Faith Callistro, student, Edgar Springs, MO

"It is both inspiring and encouraging. The love of God shines through Rob's life like the sun's ray through the kingdom."

—Kathy Brandt, Minister of Education & Outreach, Salem Avenue Baptist Church, Rolla, MO

"I enjoy behind-the-scenes stories. *The Reliever* gives a look behind the scenes in baseball and a man's journey in coming to know Jesus personally."

—Bruce Cook, Camp Ministry, Salem, MO

THE RELIEVER

MY JOURNEY FROM PITCHER TO PREACHER

ROB CALLISTRO

Published by
Innovo Publishing LLC
www.innovopublishing.com
1-888-546-2111

Providing Full-Service Publishing Services for
Christian Authors, Artists & Organizations: Hardbacks, Paperbacks,
eBooks, Audiobooks, Music & Film

THE RELIEVER
My Journey From Pitcher to Preacher

Library of Congress Control Number: 2015943131
ISBN 13: 978-1-61314-283-7

Cover Design & Interior Layout: Innovo Publishing LLC

Printed in the United States of America
U.S. Printing History

First Edition: July 2015

THE RELIEVER

MY JOURNEY FROM PITCHER TO PREACHER

DEDICATION

First, I want to say thank you to my Lord and Savior, Jesus Christ! For twenty-six years, I lived my life in a very selfish way, but You never gave up on me. You always had a plan for my life, and for that I am eternally grateful.

Eight months after I gave my life to Jesus, God brought a beautiful Christian woman into my life, and from the moment I saw her, I knew this was the one God sent my way. I will not serve in ministry without Jill. She has shown me what the love of God looks like as a godly wife, mother, and best friend!

I dedicate this book to our son, Robby, sixteen, and our daughter, Faith, thirteen. They are truly blessings sent from God, and I thank God for their encouragement and love in life and in ministry as well.

I also want to thank God for my dad, Gene, my mom, Peggy, mom #2 Carolyn, and all my other sisters and brothers. I also want to dedicate this book to my sister, Dena, for all the love and support she gave me. I thank God for all of you.

I do want to thank all of my wife's family for always showing me what a Christian family looks like, a real godly commitment.

I dedicate this book to all my former players and coaches and brothers and sisters in the ministry! May the Lord Jesus bless y'all right now!

FOREWORD

I love baseball and I love Jesus. My friend, Rob Callistro, does too. There truly is so much within the game of baseball that mirrors a life of faithfully following Jesus—the grind of a season, the triumph of winning, the joy of participating, the opportunity to try again after failing, and the sense of mission and community found among teammates. Rob has a heart for people and a desire that people hear the transformative Gospel story. That is why he is sharing his story with you. Rob's story and Jesus' story continue to inspire me, and I know they each will inspire you, as well. May you know the incredible pursuing grace of Jesus. May God bless you today and all days as you pursue life, Jesus, and baseball!

—Nolan Porter

READY OR NOT, HERE I COME!

1st Inning: Where It All Began

I was born on September 25, 1969, in Walnut Creek, California, to my dad, Gene; mom, Peggy; and one older sister, Dena. We grew up in Concord, California, and had a great childhood.

My dad and I were close, still are. I have always admired him for his dedication and commitment to his family. He always challenged me to work hard, and to this day I can hear him telling me, "Quit standing around and work!" My definition of work was always different than his. My love and passion has always been baseball.

I have wonderful memories of growing up with Dena. Sure, we fought at times, but the love was always there. When my dad caught us fighting, he would stand us face-to-face—actually nose-to-nose—and tie his belt around our waists. By the time the belt was fastened, we were laughing and would forget what we were even fighting about!

Setting the Goal

When I was five years old, I remember telling my parents that when I grew up I wanted to play baseball just like the guys on television. I think at some point, every little boy aspires to be like the athlete he sees on TV.

I was always playing with some type of ball. I must have broken a window in almost every house in our neighborhood with those balls. I remember spending hours upon hours throwing a tennis ball against my garage door, the neighbor's retaining wall, or a handball court at the local park. I would imagine myself as one of baseball's pitching greats. I would attempt to copy their style and body movements when I threw the ball. I loved everything about playing baseball—the smell of a baseball, the smell of the glove after oiling it, the smell of the dirt, the smell of the grass, the practices, the games.

My dad was the reason I started playing baseball at seven. I have always cherished the memories of playing catch in the street in front of our house, and at practices and games, as he coached a few of my teams when I was young.

My dad threw a no-hitter when he was in Little League, and his game was heard live on the radio. So the love for baseball and pitching was passed down to me.

GETTING STARTED

2ND INNING: CHILDHOOD MEMORIES

You're Out!

Whil When I was seven, I played for the Tigers. One day when I came up to bat, I hit it way in the outfield. As I ran to first base, the coach said, "Robby, run to second base!" Now, I did what every base runner should *not* do; I stopped at second base and looked around. My coach yelled, "Robby, keep running!" So I ran to third base, and as I approached, my coach yelled, "Robby, run home, run home!" As I continued to run, I thought, *I'm about to get a home run!* Just as I was getting close to home plate, the catcher caught the ball just as I slid into home. He tagged me and the umpire yelled, "You're out!"

Being called out would have been fine except that my dad was the umpire. To this day, I can call my dad and say that I was safe, and he would say that I'm still out!

Changeup

My sister and I were riding in the car with our mom when she told us something that would change our way of life forever. My mom said, "Your dad and me are getting a divorce!" I laughed and asked, "What does that mean?" She said, "We won't be living together as a family."

When my parents divorced, my sister and I lived with our mom for a short time, and then we moved back in with our dad. I was raised in the same house and in the same neighborhood my whole childhood life. My heart hurt every time I spent the weekend with my dad because he stayed in the house I grew up in. Each time I walked into my old room and saw baseball bats and baseballs on my bedroom floor, I wanted to cry. To me, it wasn't about choosing my dad over my mom; it was about living where I felt comfortable.

My Favorite Baseball Team

I was on the Pacific Coast League (PCL) Oaks team, and my dad was the head coach. PCL was the name of the ballpark. Our uniforms were white with orange trim and an orange logo of an acorn. It seemed like before every game my dad and I would drive around town and pick up many of our players. We were a very close-knit team.

We cared about each other because we had a lot of things in common. Many of my teammates had parents who were divorced also. In some of the games, I would play catcher for three innings and then I would pitch three innings. In one game, while playing catcher, several foul tips hit off the players' bats right into my right shoulder. My shoulder swelled up, but I looked at it as my badge of honor. After the games, it was customary that we would go out for pizza as a team. Many times, I remember wearing an ice bag on my shoulder at the pizza place.

One of my greatest baseball memories was when the Oaks' regular season ended, and we played a well-known Little League team from Danville, California. They pulled into our baseball parking lot in limousines, carrying with them practice uniforms as well as game uniforms. We had only one set of uniforms—some players had hot chocolate stains on theirs while others only had one orange stirrup. We looked like a bunch of misfit baseball players in comparison to the other team. But our team loved to play baseball together, and we would play hard with an undying commitment. We not only won the game that day, but we beat them 10 to 0!

My stepfather, Manny, often personally challenged me by talking to me through the dugout fence. He'd tell me that if I struck out a certain number of hitters, he would take me out for pizza. Let's just say that I ate a lot of pizza growing up!

I JUST LOVED
PLAYING BASEBALL!

3RD INNING: SNACK SHACK SATURDAYS

Snack shack Saturdays always started out with a loud, "Boo!" That was my dad's way of waking me up and getting me ready for my baseball games.

My dad would take me to ¼ lb Big Burger in Concord for a hearty breakfast before my Saturday games. I remember the owner/cook, who always wore a food-stained apron, would come over to our table to say hello and give me some encouragement about the game.

I played at PCL from the ages of ten through thirteen. I loved my Saturdays at the ballpark. For me, it didn't matter if we won or lost; I just loved playing. Many times, I would look up from the pitcher's mound and take a quick glance at the bleachers to see if my grandma showed up (unannounced) to watch me play.

I would spend all day hanging out at the ballpark. I watched as many games as I could, getting up periodically to make a trip to the snack shack for hot dogs, soda, and candy. Did I overeat on junk food? Naturally!

When all the games were over, or if it was getting dark, I walked to my grandma's house, which was only a half mile from the field. This was a very special time in my life—spending time with Grandma Lila "Sparkles" Callistro. This was our baseball season tradition. I would spend the night at Grandma Sparkles' house; sometimes we'd order pizza and sometimes she would make me dinner. We would watch her favorite movies starring Clark Gable, Lana Turner, John Wayne, Jimmy Stewart, or Ronald Reagan, just to name a few. I loved spending those days and nights talking with Grandma Sparkles about baseball, telling her about my recent games, and sharing with her my dreams of one day playing professional baseball.

Left: Rob's youth baseball picture for the PCL Broncos
Right: Rob's youth baseball picture for the PCL Senators

I Have a Surprise for You

Grandma Sparkles surprised me one year (I was seventeen) when she showed me a scrapbook that she had been working on since I was younger. It had newspaper articles about me from different Northern California area newspapers, along with plenty of individual and team photos. Some of the pictures I had never seen before. That scrapbook meant a lot to me, especially since it was such an amazing gift from my grandma.

I asked my grandma to tell me what my grandpa would be like if he were alive and able to attend my baseball games. She said he would've worn a shirt with my team colors and number. He would have been so proud of me. She also told me that he coached my dad when my dad played baseball as a young boy. That made me smile.

I CAUGHT BASEBALL FEVER.

4th Inning: Dreaming Big

My grandma was great at listening and encouraging her grandkids and their dreams. She showed such interest in every detail of baseball. She was one of the first people to ever take me to an Oakland Athletics game. One of her close friends usually went with us. We'd go to the game on BART (Bay Area Rapid Transit), which would take us directly to the A's stadium. Whenever I knew I would be going to an A's game, the anticipation was almost excruciating. I'd count the train stops as we got closer to the stadium. When we arrived at the Oakland A's Coliseum, we would walk over the bridge connecting BART to the stadium. I would walk faster when I heard the A's announcer on the PA and saw the players from both teams on the field getting ready. Walking to our seats, I'd hear the food and beverage vendors shouting, "Hot dogs, peanuts, Crackerjacks, Coke, and ice cream!"

During one game in particular, when we sat behind the home dugout about twenty rows up, the batter hit a line drive (foul ball) right at my grandma's face, and I put my hand up to protect her. The ball hit my hand, and let me tell you my hand hurt for many days! I did not actually catch the baseball as a souvenir.

Oftentimes, my dad would buy me a hat or some kind of a souvenir from the game. I loved going to professional baseball games; the smell of the grass and watching the players play at such a high skill level was amazing. One year, I remember sitting near the opposing team's bullpen, which gave me several opportunities to meet and watch pitchers from different teams. I would watch coaches talk with pitchers as pitchers warmed up, and I would imagine what they were talking about.

I loved watching professional games in person and on television. As a teenager, I focused on pitchers and spent hours practicing pitching.

Rob pitching for the Junior Varsity Team at Concord High School

Rob hitting for the Junior Varsity Team at Concord High School

I dreamt of pitching in the Oakland A's Coliseum in front of thousands of people. I imitated many of my childhood baseball heroes by imagining game situations and pitching to imaginary hitters. I also imitated certain pitchers' motions, mechanics, and deliveries of the pitch. As time went on, I developed my own pitching style.

One year, we had a former professional baseball player speak at our high school during an assembly. He said that he learned how to pitch, not just throw. That may not mean much to some people, but it was sage advice. Since then, I have always focused on pitching, not just throwing. I would always work on different types of pitches in different game situations and counts.

I had the great honor of playing baseball with some outstanding baseball players during youth baseball, high school, summer ball, and all-star tournament teams. I remember Tony Dress played first base. Tony was, and is, one of the most passionate baseball players I have ever met. His love and enthusiasm for baseball was incredible, and he made it easy for me to want to play baseball with him. Just like in the football movie *The Blind Side*, Tony was that baseball friend who always watched out and protected my blind side! For many of the guys that I grew up playing baseball with, we never focused on winning; we just loved to play hard and winning just happened.

My first no-hitter was in high school against Liberty High School. I struck out twelve hitters while walking one. We won that game. I had no idea that I even threw a no-hitter until our head coach, Gary Luoma, congratulated me in front of the whole team. When I threw my second no-hitter, I was aware of it. We played at California High School, and it was a very windy day. Many players made some incredible plays that day.

I did walk a few hitters, who then advanced a few bases. I balked in a run[1] from my body swaying on the pitcher's mound.

During my junior and senior years in high school, I loved coming home after school and going straight to the mailbox to see what colleges sent me letters of interest. It was so gratifying to receive calls from college coaches and professional scouts. Arizona State University was interested in me for a while. At the time, they were playing in the College World Series in Omaha, Nebraska. The recruiting coordinator called me after one of their games to discuss my future plans, and even though my goal was to play professional baseball, I loved that they were interested in me. The recruiting coordinator from Arizona State University called me during their World Series. He asked, me if I had watched their game that day. Getting that phone call was cool. I thought about playing college baseball at ASU.

My dad and I went on a recruiting trip to St. Mary's College in Moraga, California. We toured the campus and attended a college basketball game where we experienced the student body's excitement during the game. After the game, we spent time talking with the coaching staff about their interest in me coming to St. Mary's College and what my role would be. I did not commit or attend St. Mary's, but the attention they showed me was pretty fun.

---

[1] A runner was on third base, and I made a body flinch, so the umpire called a "balk," which means the runner scored from third base.

So close I can taste it!

5TH INNING: THE DREAM GETTING CLOSER

One professional scout that showed years of commitment and interest in me was Mr. Pete Jones of the Seattle Mariners baseball organization. I remember seeing him at summer tournaments beginning when I was around thirteen years old. He followed me and showed interest all the way through my freshman year at Diablo Valley Junior College (DVJC). Pete spent hundreds of hours on the road driving to my games, and he must have spent just as much time watching me pitch. He had a faithful commitment to my future in baseball.

At the conclusion of my high-school career, Pete Jones told me that the Seattle Mariners selected me in the 43rd round of the 1988 major-league baseball player draft. I was so excited! In that one moment, all of my boyhood dreams had come true. I thought, *I'm going to be a professional baseball player!* Those thoughts were short lived, as I found out very soon that I was a draft-and-follow player. Meaning, I was drafted by the Seattle Mariners, and they would follow me closely as I played at a local junior college. I signed a draft-and-follow contract with Seattle, giving them rights to sign me first if they liked what they saw within a year. During my year at DVJC, I was able to play with my cousin Tim Wettstein; he was one of the best shortstops and purest hitters I had ever played with. He taught me how to play with passion and to never give in or to never give up on the baseball field. I always felt that I had a front row seat to the best baseball player! His nickname for me was "Fats"—I was a pretty skinny baseball player at that time in my life.

Tim was one of the members of the Diablo Valley Junior College baseball "Bash brothers." The other members were catcher Mike Murphy, who ended up playing with the Houston Astros; third baseman

Caesar Medina, who won the California Junior College batting title; and second baseman Andy Boom. Our baseball team at DVJC was one of the most talented teams I have ever been a part of. We played for head coach, Steve Ward; he was very intense. The way he coached was by example, and he demanded hard work and respect. I enjoyed playing for him, even if it was only one year.

A Confusing Time

My time at DVJC was a confusing time in my life. I had such a desire to play professional baseball that I did not see the other opportunities around me, like education.

I was very narrow minded and selfish. My identity was in pitching, but off the baseball field I felt lost and confused. The Bible says, in 1 Timothy 4:7, *Have nothing to do with godless myths and old wives' tales; rather, train yourself to be godly.* I never knew that God gave me the gifts and talent to play baseball! He gave me countless opportunities to give Him the glory that is due His name.

At the beginning of the 1989 baseball season at DVJC, we traveled to play a game in San Francisco, California. The Seattle Mariners' scout, Pete Jones, and a regional scouting director came to the game to check on my progress at the start of the season. As I was warming up in the bullpen, getting ready to pitch, my arm started hurting. In all my years of pitching, I had experienced some pain, tightness, and soreness before, but I had never felt pain like this before. I tried to throw a fastball, but the baseball only traveled halfway between me and the catcher. I acted like the ball slipped out of my hand, so the catcher threw the ball back to me. I attempted another fastball with the same results. I was very freaked out at what was happening so I said to my catcher, "I'm warmed up and ready to pitch!"

He asked me, "Are you okay?"

I lied and said, "Yeah, I'm good."

I was excited about the Seattle Mariners' representatives being at my game, but I was also very scared about the pain I was feeling in my arm. What would they think when they found out?

When the game started, I sat there in the dugout, as we hit first. All I could think about was the pain in my arm and that the Mariners were there to check on my progress. When it was my time to take the mound and pitch, I felt okay as I warmed up. Then the incredible pain came back. I threw a fastball that bounced in front of the catcher. The next pitch landed right in front of the pitcher's mound. My face revealed my pain and discomfort. The head coach ran out to me and asked if I was all right. I told him no, the pain was unbearable.

I could see the look of disappointment on many faces, including the scouts. I was very worried about my baseball future with the Seattle Mariners.

I found out the next day that my arm was fatigued, so the team doctor put my arm in a sling and told me for the next month my arm needed total rest. He said I could not use my right arm for anything! A month later I returned to full pitching duty. I had to spend some time getting my arm back to full strength, but I did not have any more arm trouble for the rest of the season. The scare of my baseball career ending was over.

During the season at DVJC our team played very well. We ended up tied for the divisional lead. We played a one game playoff in which we won on a game-winning hit by my cousin Tim. Like I said, he was a great hitter.

At the end of the baseball season, I had a choice between coming back to DVJC for another year or playing summer ball in the Alaskan league or signing a professional contract with the Seattle Mariners baseball team.

WOW!

6TH INNING: THE DREAM COMES TRUE

On June 12, 1989, my dad and I met with Pete Jones and another representative from the Seattle Mariners baseball team. We discussed the details of the contract, and I signed, becoming a professional baseball player for the Seattle Mariners! I received congratulations from family, former coaches, players, and even neighbors. After all the years spent practicing and playing games with various teams and players, my dream had finally come true!

When I was five years old, I set a goal for myself to become a professional baseball player, and now I had accomplished just that.

Is This It?

I stood alone in the kitchen of the house where I grew up. I leaned against the kitchen counter thinking, *Is this it?* I spent countless hours practicing and playing baseball with my dad, friends, family, and many teams over the years. I spent years watching baseball games on TV and in person, and now I was a professional baseball player. So shouldn't I be happier?

I was so confused. On one hand I was so excited and happy about reaching my goal of playing professional baseball, but on the other hand I felt like I was missing something. I felt scared and nervous, not in my ability as a baseball player but in me as a person.

The Bible says, in 1 Timothy 4:7–8, *Have nothing to do with godless myths and old wives' tales; rather, train yourself to be godly. For physical training is of some value, but godliness has value for all things, holding promise for both the present life and the life to come.*

I never realized that God gave me the gifts and talent to play baseball! He also gave me countless opportunities to give Him the glory. For the first twenty-six years of my life, I believed that if I became a professional baseball player, I would have all of the happiness in the world and I would have peace in my life. I was so wrong! I believed a lie. I believed a godless myth!

Confused About Happiness

Now, I want you to hear me when I say that I had many happy moments in my baseball life, like being drafted by the Seattle Mariners and signing a contract with them, and later the Chicago White Sox. I was happy when great things were happening for me. I was confused because great things were happening, but on the inside something was missing and I had no idea what it was.

Arizona Mariners

I soon left for Tempe, Arizona, and played in the Arizona rookie league[2] for the Arizona Mariners. Sitting on the airplane in Oakland, bound for Arizona, I wore sunglasses, not because I was trying to be cool but because I was fighting back the tears of fear. I was fearful because I was leaving home for the first time, and I was leaving the known for the unknown. I had lived in the same house for nineteen years, and now I was not only going to live in a new city in a new state but I was also going to be a professional baseball player. I thought that the Seattle Mariners expected something from me for giving me an opportunity to

---

[2] The rookie league is professional baseball, under the umbrella of the major leagues.

play baseball. I had no idea that it was God giving me the opportunity to play professional baseball, with all of the glory and honor due His name!

I had a great summer playing for the Arizona Mariners; I had success on the baseball field as a starting pitcher. My pitching coach was Brian Price. That was his first year of coaching in professional baseball, and now he is the manager of the Cincinnati Reds. In 1989, I learned more about who I was as a starting pitcher than any other time in my life. He taught me how to pitch by teaching me pitch selection and how to read the hitters' tendencies (their movements, balance, and strengths). On game days, he would drive the starting pitcher to the game so he could talk about how to prepare for the game. These were some of the most important days of my baseball life. He coached by showing personal attention, and it improved my game. It encouraged and challenged me to be my best. On the pitcher's mound I felt very confident in my ability and talent.

My best friend flew to Arizona to watch me pitch. The days he was with me the weather reached about 110 to 118 degrees. One of the games he watched me pitch was against the Arizona Brewers, the Milwaukee Brewers' rookie ball team. During the game, I noticed that my friend was changing seats all throughout the game. He said he was so hot that he had to keep moving around the ballpark. We won that game, and my friend reminded me that I threw a no-hitter. That season I led the league in strikeouts, and I finished fifth in earned run average. I was even an All-Star selection. I had a successful first season with the Arizona Mariners.

My first year in the minor leagues[3] was a very difficult time. When I wasn't on the baseball field, I found myself trying to be someone that I wasn't. I tried so hard to fit in with other players that sometimes I would

---

[3] The minor league is professional baseball, under the umbrella of the major leagues.

exaggerate and tell lies to try to make myself appear better than I was. I understood that players needed to focus on their baseball careers, but selfishness, pride, and backbiting occurred when players only thought of themselves.

Picking Up Where I Left Off

I traveled back to Concord, California, after my first summer playing professional baseball. I spent the off-season physically training my body, but I also spent that time training myself to party with my friends. I wasn't of legal age to drink alcohol, but I had been drinking since I was around fourteen years old. The off-season seemed like it went by so fast. I felt ready to return to playing baseball, but the expectations and the pressure to succeed were very real.

I left for the Seattle Mariners' spring-training facility in Tempe, Arizona, in March of 1990. I spent the next four months in what is called "extended spring training." I was promoted to the Bellingham Mariners[4] for the rest of the season. I had a very difficult season in Bellingham, Washington. For the first time in my life, I started to question my ability and identity as a baseball pitcher. I didn't feel like I was receiving good instruction from my pitching coach, and I was struggling. I was confused about my mechanics, and I began to wonder about my identity. I doubted my ability as a pitcher for the very first time in my life, and this scared me deeply.

---

[4] The Bellingham Mariners are a minor league team in the Seattle Mariners' organization.

My Worst Game Ever

We traveled to Eureka, Washington, to play the Eureka Giants. I was now pitching as a reliever. During the game, our starting pitcher was getting hit pretty hard (giving up a lot of hits and runs), the Giants were beating us 12–0, and there were over seventeen thousand people in the stands. I was called on to warm up, and I entered the game with no outs in the fifth inning. While warming up on the game mound, the first hitter stepped in the batter's box. On the first pitch I threw him, he smacked the ball over the right-field fence for a home run! The second hitter stepped in the batter's box, and he hit the ball over the left-field fence for another home run! You can imagine that I felt like hiding in a hole. Believe it or not, the third hitter hit the ball over the center-field fence for yet another home run for the team.

Three home runs to three hitters without one out. I wanted out of there. I had never been so embarrassed on a baseball field before.

Our team manager came out to the mound, pulled me to the side, and said a few choice words to me. I walked into the dugout feeling like an embarrassment and a failure. When I sat down on the bench, no one—not even one teammate or a coach—said anything to me. It was like no one wanted to be around me. I felt like I had a curse!

The Bible says in Psalm 51:5, *Surely I was sinful at birth, sinful from the time my mother conceived me.* Romans 3:10, 23 says, *"There is no one righteous, not even one;" . . . for all have sinned and fall short of the glory of God . . .*

The Long Ride Home

After the game, we sat on the team bus for a while before we traveled the two hours back to Bellingham, Washington. One of the other pitchers, who sat behind me, handed me his Walkman so I could stop thinking about my worst pitching performance ever. I just listened to music as we drove back home.

I realized years later that I did have a curse, and that curse was unrepentant sin. John 3:16–17 says, *For God so loved the world that he gave his one and only Son, that whoever believes in him shall not perish but have eternal life. For God did not send his Son into the world to condemn the world, but to save the world through him.* First Timothy 4:7–8 says, *Have nothing to do with godless myths and old wives' tales; rather, train yourself to be godly. For physical training is of some value, but godliness has value for all things, holding promise for both the present life and the life to come.*

I Get to Pitch Where?

We traveled to Seattle, Washington, to the play a game in the Kingdome—the former home stadium of the Seattle Mariners. The stadium lights would turn on a few at a time so our eyes could adjust to the lighting. We walked into the home clubhouse and visited with the major-league players. Personally, I was interested in talking with the pitchers. I asked them questions pertaining to their roles as starters or relievers. One pitcher I really enjoyed talking to was Billy Swift; he threw a major-league sinker, and that was my goal—to throw a sinker in the major leagues. I played in a game against the Eugene Emeralds (KC Royals affiliate), and I was scheduled to pitch in the seventh inning. I struck out three players, and I hit a batter while walking two other players. I will never forget pitching in the Seattle Kingdome.

Rob pitching in the Kingdome, 1991

I WORSHIPED
BASEBALL, AND
BASEBALL BECAME A
SNARE TO ME.

7TH INNING: TAKE YOUR BASEBALL AND GO

I left for the Seattle Mariners' spring-training facility in Tempe, Arizona, in March of 1991. I arrived at about eight in the morning. As I approached a member of the Seattle Mariners front office staff, he asked if he could talk with me. I said yes. We walked into a portable building that sat next to our clubhouse. The development director wasted no time. He slid a piece of paper toward me on the table and asked me to sign it. I asked what it was and he said, "We are releasing you from your contract." I wasn't familiar with a "release" so I asked what that was. He said that I had done everything they had ever asked of me, and much more, but they just didn't have room for me in their organization!

So I got to take my ball and go home!

The Pain Gets Even Worse

As if getting released wasn't bad enough . . . As I was signing my release form, I noticed a name that was circled at the bottom of the page. I asked about that name. He said, "That is the name of our team doctor. You see, some young men commit suicide after getting released." That blew my mind!

I often wonder how God feels when a person takes his own life. Young men that He gave life, breath, gifts, and the talent to play professional baseball. Why is it they are committing suicide after getting released?

As I went back to my hotel, I was devastated! My whole life and identity was as a baseball pitcher. I placed all of my hope, trust . . . everything in my life was as a baseball pitcher. So what do I do now?

One of the hardest moments for me after being released was calling my dad to share the news with him. I called my dad from the hotel lobby. Fighting back tears, I told him I had just been released from the Mariners, I was flying home, and that I needed him to pick me up at the airport.

A fellow teammate, who had also been released, and I got together to say our good-byes; we had been released the same morning.

The Airport Pickup

My dad picked me up in the baggage claim area at Oakland International Airport. I don't really remember what we said because I was in such a fog. I'm sure my dad didn't know what to say to me. He didn't place any demands, pressure, or expectations on my baseball career. I placed the expectations and the pressure to succeed in my baseball career on myself. I felt embarrassment, humiliation, failure, anger, frustration, regret, and doubts. I felt so much pain because every bit of my identity was as a baseball player, and now I found myself wondering, *What will I do now?*

I Kept Trying

A few weeks after I returned home, I received a phone call from a manager of an independent (professional baseball) team called the Pocatello Pioneers. They told me they wanted me to travel to Pocatello, Idaho, and try out for their team. The season would start in June, and we would play through August. I made the team and began pitching in the starting rotation again. I was happy to be pitching in professional baseball again, even if it was for an independent team. I had a great time playing and traveling with my new teammates. We weren't very good as a team, but many of the players worked hard and tried to play well enough so that we could sign contracts with a major-league baseball organization. I spent the summer as their starting pitcher. I worked hard to return to the pitcher I once was. When I played for the Seattle Mariners, I was a relief pitcher, which means that I was available on a daily basis. I was used as a seventh-inning guy who came into the ball game to throw my sinker and try to get the hitter to hit into a double play. Now that I was back as a starting pitcher, I would pitch every fifth game.

It Happened So Quickly

We were winning 4 to 1 in the seventh inning. The opposing team had a runner on second base with zero outs. I was instructed by our manager that if the hitter bunted the ball down the third-base line that the third baseman would field the ball and throw the runner out at first base. I threw the pitch, and the hitter bunted the ball in the air between the pitcher's mound and third base. I dove for the ball, and as I hit the ground my lower back popped! I stood back up, but I could not stand up straight. I felt numbness from the middle of my legs into my stomach area.

The next day, I was taken to a back doctor for an MRI. The doctor revealed a fracture in my lower back. The doctor walked into the room and placed a shiny scalpel and a shiny five-pound dumbbell on the bed next to me. He said, "Pick one." I said, "What?" He said, "You can choose surgery, but surgery won't help you. You need to go home and start lifting weights to get your body stronger."

Damaged Goods

I finished the season injured. I went back home with the label of "damaged goods." At that time in the world of professional baseball, if you were released or hurt, you were labeled "damaged goods." I have now been both released from professional baseball and hurt. No professional baseball organization wants a player that is damaged.

I wonder how God feels about His creation being identified as damaged goods? God created everyone in this world. He desires fellowship with all of His children. That means that God wants a personal relationship with every person all around the world. He created you and me with gifts and talents; He gives us countless opportunities to give Him the glory and the praise to live our lives to please Him. Psalm 115:1 says, *Not to us, Lord, not to us, but to your name be the glory, because of your love and faithfulness.*

Until this point in my life, I never knew that I was to give all the glory to God and that He wanted a personal relationship with me. Did you know God wants to have a personal relationship with you? I had been trying to make myself happy by my own efforts. I had placed so much pressure on myself to succeed, and I could not make myself completely happy no matter what I did! Why? Because I learned that life is not about me.

Self-Destructive Lifestyle

I spent the next three and a half years living exactly the same way I had always trained myself to live—selfishly! I became a trainer at a gym so I could work and workout about six days a week. I also worked as a bouncer in a nightclub, and I taught pitching and hitting lessons at an indoor facility. I wanted to keep my identity as a professional baseball player so badly that I traveled to many major-league baseball tryouts.

On one road trip, three of my buddies and I drove from Northern California to the Phoenix, Arizona area to try out for the Arizona Diamondbacks. To give you an idea of what some baseball tryouts are like, they are called "cattle calls." At the beginning, you sign in and they give you a number that you attach to your back. You stretch a little, run a little, play catch, and wait around a little, all depending on the position you play. Sooner or later they call you to try out. After you are finished, you wait a little longer, hoping to be signed to play professional baseball.

I spent days, weeks, and even months typing, stuffing, and mailing many letters to major-league baseball scouts, asking them for tryouts to play for their team. A scout from one professional organization called me and invited me to travel down to Southern California for a one-on-one tryout. I was excited. Cattle call tryouts are with about hundred other ball players looking to sign a professional contract. This time, it was just me. I asked my dad to buy me an airplane ticket to go to the tryout.

I arrived at a park in Southern California where I met the scout who invited me. I soon figured out that this wasn't a one-on-one tryout like I thought. Anyway, I pitched against a few local players. I pitched well but not well enough that day, and I didn't get to sign a contract with the organization.

As the days turned into months and the months to years, I turned to alcohol to numb the hurt and pain that I was feeling. I was hurting inside, and all I wanted was some kind of relief for my pain, but I didn't know what the answer was. As I was turned down by one team after another, I felt rejected and alone. My identity for years was in a baseball, and the rejections took me down a very dangerous path. I wanted to be back in professional baseball, and I was willing to do whatever it took to feel accepted again. I kept hearing from people in the baseball world that a baseball player who gets released needs to show the decision makers something different than when the player got released. What I heard was, "Get bigger, faster, and stronger."

So I worked very hard in the gym to get bigger and stronger, and I hoped to throw faster on the mound. Nothing seemed to work for me, so I bought some steroids to help me. I was so scared to inject the steroids that I asked a friend of mine to help me. The first night I laid in bed with my heart racing, and I could not go to sleep. I was too scared to keep using steroids, so I quit. For years, I would not listen to any advice from family or friends about my baseball career so I spent many months working out in the gym, teaching baseball, and throwing and pitching with friends, just hoping for another opportunity to play professional ball.

Another Baseball Opportunity

A scout from the Chicago White Sox called me and asked me if I wanted to try out. I met him at a field in San Francisco, California. I pitched for about half an hour, and he called me later that day and said that the Chicago White Sox wanted to give me an opportunity to go to spring training in Sarasota, Florida, in a few days. I flew to Sarasota, Florida, and I spent the first three months of 1995 working out in their spring-training facility. At the conclusion of spring training, I made the Prince William Cannons, a former minor-league team[5] that played in the Carolina league. I pitched in the bullpen as a reliever. Once again, I found myself struggling with my identity as a pitcher. On April 26, 1995, I walked

---

[5] Prince William Cannons were a minor-league team in the Chicago White Sox organization.

into the clubhouse to pack my baseball bag for our road trip when I was called into the manager's office. The manager told me to close the door and to have a seat. He said, "I'm not sure what happened last night, but you have been released from your contract."

I shook his hand, thanked him for the opportunity to play, and walked out of his office. One of the players told me to hurry up and get my stuff because the bus was leaving soon. I told him that I just got released. He thought I was kidding. When he realized I was serious, he gave me a quick hug and wished me luck.

Reality Check

I went back to my apartment and called my baseball agent to tell him that I just got released from the Chicago White Sox. He said, "Don't travel home yet." He said that since I got released during the season, I may get picked up (signed) by another major-league team. He said he would call me soon. I spent the next three days sitting around my apartment wondering what was going on. I couldn't wait any longer so I called him. It was a good thing I did. He told me he could not represent me any longer! He said that he did everything he could for me but that he wouldn't be doing anything else.

Two Times Is Enough

After that, I felt sure I did not want to continue trying to make baseball a career. Again, the hardest thing for me to do was to call my dad because of the expectations I put on myself. Even at the age of twenty-five, there was still a part of me that wanted to make my dad proud of me, like when I was a seven-year-old boy pitching for the first time in my first game.

What Is My Identity?

I traveled back home and I did what I had always trained myself to do. I called my friends, and we went to bars and nightclubs every weekend. I tried to drink my pain away.

The Crash

On Halloween night in 1995, I went to a family party at my sister's house. Then I went to another party with a few friends. People asked me how baseball was going, and I told them I wasn't playing anymore. I acted like everything was okay, but it wasn't. I drank a lot of alcohol that night; I was trying to drink away the failure and disappointment that I was feeling from being released from professional baseball. At the end of the party, I got the keys to a friend's car. In my mind, I was going to turn on the stereo so everyone outside could hear it, but instead I started the car, put the car in gear with my foot on the accelerator, and the car started racing down the long, steep driveway. With my left leg hanging out of the driver's side door, suddenly the car struck a tree, the airbag deployed, and the car split right down the middle! Some of my friends and my cousin were standing up at the top of the driveway watching the whole thing, and they told me later they thought I was dead for sure. The airbag is what physically saved my life. I then climbed out the passenger side and I lay on the road for a few minutes; I didn't really know what had just happened because I was so drunk. One of my friends drove me to my sister's house before the cops could come and arrest me for driving under the influence. I was living at my sister's house and sleeping on her couch.

The next day I went to the hospital to get checked out. The doctor said that I just needed to rest a few days.

My drinking did not stop. For a while, partying with my so-called friends at bars and nightclubs was a weekend thing, but my weekend drinking turned to daily drinking, and my daily drinking turned in to trying harder drugs. I was lost and hurting and nothing I did seemed to fill the void in my heart. Ecclesiastes 3:11 says, *He has made everything beautiful in its time. He has also set eternity in the human heart; yet no one can fathom what God has done from beginning to end.*

God has placed eternity on the hearts of every one of us; we all have a void in our hearts without a personal relationship with God!

I Was Broken

I woke up one morning and looked at myself in the mirror, and I didn't like what I saw. I had lost a lot of weight from the endless partying, drinking, and using drugs—partying with people I thought were my friends. The truth was they were drunk and high just like me. Like the saying goes: "Misery loves company."

God Has a Plan

John 6:44 says, *"No one can come to me unless the Father who sent me draws them, and I will raise them up at the last day."*

All I can say is what happened next is God's divine and miraculous plan!

I was very physically and mentally worn out, totally exhausted from the life I was living. I was so disappointed in myself that I literally could not even look at myself in a mirror for very long.

I rented a hotel room for a weekend so I could lie in bed, watch television, and just be alone. I don't remember telling anyone that I had gotten a hotel room. I was hurting beyond my own understanding.

I was lying in bed watching television when the phone rang. It rang about four times then stopped ringing. I thought, *No one knows I'm here so that call wasn't for me.* The phone rang again and around the third or fourth ring I answered it. My mother was on the other end of the phone, asking me how I was doing. I lied and said okay, but she knew I wasn't okay; mothers just know. I wasted no time in asking my mom her thoughts about me moving to Missouri where she was living, and she said, "How fast can you get here?"

I now know that God was drawing me to Himself! He loved me and wanted a personal relationship with me. He knew I was hurting by the sin in my life, and it was tearing me apart from the inside out. God's plan for me included going to my dad's house and telling him exactly what I had been doing. One of the most difficult moments of my life happened next. I call it turning myself in to my dad. All I remember was breaking my dad's heart! He took one look at me and said, "What did you do to yourself?" I told him that I had been spending a lot of time partying; I was doing drugs and drinking a lot of alcohol.

Getting Away

I told my dad I was moving to Waynesville, Missouri, to live with my mom and her husband. My dad and I agreed that I needed a change of scenery. At the conclusion of our time together, there were tears and heartbreak. I loved my dad and my stepmom. She always called herself mom #2. She was a great mom; she helped me in many ways during the darkest times in my life. She was very loving and did not have a condemning spirit. I have always been very grateful for her love and support.

I loved living in Concord, California, and I would miss my family and friends, but I needed to get away and heal—physically, mentally, emotionally, and spiritually—from my self-destructive behavior.

FOR GOD SO LOVED ME!

8TH INNING: BEING DRAWN

I left around six in the morning from Concord, California, heading to Waynesville, Missouri. After about ten hours of driving, I arrived in Needles, California, on the border of Arizona. I rented a hotel room for the night. I planned to get up and start driving at about six in the morning, but God had other plans for me. I had a pizza delivered, and I watched baseball on television.

I fell asleep and woke up sometime later. I popped out of bed, took a quick shower, packed my bag, and got into the car. I headed to the gas station to fill up before I started my day of driving. I finally looked at a clock and realized that it was the middle of the night! My plan was to leave at 6:00 a.m. But at that moment I just felt like I needed to go. I felt excited, like a young boy going to Disneyland for the first time.

I finally arrived in central Missouri at a truck stop restaurant near Waynesville, Missouri. I called my mom, and she gave me directions to her house. About twenty minutes later, I arrived at my mom's house. She came out to greet me with a big hug. The first thing I asked her was, "Is there a good church in town?" Her eyes got big and she stared at me in utter surprise. I wasn't raised in the church, and I only remember attending one church service in my life.

I Had Never Heard

I was so happy to be in a new place where I knew no one (except my mom) and no one knew me. For the first time in a long time, it felt like I was in the right place.

On Sunday morning, my mom and I went to church together for the first time that I can ever remember. We went to First Baptist Church of Waynesville, Missouri. After the church service, I met Pastor Bill. Bill and I just clicked, and we became really good friends. He took an interest in me and showed me what a godly man looked like. Bill said that he had never known a professional baseball player so he was interested in what that life was all about—the real stories, not the stuff you hear on TV. We talked for about forty-five minutes, and then Bill asked if I would listen to him share something. He was the first person to ever share the gospel of Jesus Christ with me. He told me the Good News that God loved me so much that He sent His Son to die for me, and that my sins are forgiven. He explained that Jesus Christ was raised to life on the third day and sits at the right hand of the Father in heaven. Jesus has conquered sin, death, and the grave for me and for the world!

For the next few weeks, I went out of my way to look for Bill. I wanted him to tell me more about this Jesus, and he did. He spent a lot of time talking with me and reading the Bible to me.

My mom gave her life to Jesus Christ about six years before my arrival to Waynesville. She spent countless hours praying for me to give my life to the Lord. She even strategically put a Bible next to my bed with a marker at Matthew 6:9–15. One of my favorite songs is "When Momma Prays." The song really spoke to my heart in a real way; it simply says, (paraphrasing) "When I was out getting drunk and partying with my friends, my mama was on her knees talking to Jesus about me; when momma prays!"

Matthew 6:9–15 says, *"This, then, is how you should pray: 'Our Father in heaven, hallowed be your name, your kingdom come, your will be done, on earth as it is in heaven. Give us today our daily bread. And forgive us our debts, as we also have forgiven our debtors. And lead us not into temptation, but deliver us from the evil one.' For if you forgive other people when they sin against you, your heavenly Father will also forgive you. But if you do not forgive others their sins, your Father will not forgive your sins."*

I had never read a Bible or prayed before, and these were the exact words I needed to be confronted with. I realized for the first time that I could have an eternal Father in heaven— *"hallowed be your name, your kingdom come, your will be done, on earth as it is in heaven. Give us today our daily bread."'*

I told God that He was above all things in my life and that I needed help from something greater than me. I asked God to give me my daily bread for that day; I was actually asking for help! *"And forgive us our debts, as we also have forgiven our debtors. And lead us not into temptation, but deliver us from the evil one.' For if you forgive other people when they sin against you, your heavenly Father will also forgive you. But if you do not forgive others their sins, your Father will not forgive your sins."*

I was experiencing God's power like I had never seen or felt before. I thought, *God has the power to forgive my debts, and I can forgive my debtors?*

Before that moment, I had never wondered why or who or where my temptations came from. I knew there was evil in the world, but I never knew the reality of the devil. It was a very heart-stirring moment for me when I realized for the first time that I had been living for the devil rather than for God, and that I needed to ask God to deliver me from evil every day so I could live a life that pleases Him, not man. I also realized for the first time that I needed to forgive the people that have hurt me so I could be forgiven by my heavenly Father, and there was no a question I wanted God to forgive me for all my sins! John 10:10 says, *The thief comes only to steal and kill and destroy; I have come that they may have life, and have it to the full.*

Night after night, I sat on my bed, read the Bible, and prayed to God. Little did I know that what I was reading was so powerful and life changing!

I spent the next few weeks reading, praying, and asking my mom, Pastor Bill, and others many questions about God, Jesus, and the Holy Spirit. I was at a very important place in my life; I was physically and mentally worn out from trying to carry the self-disappointment from my baseball career and the burden from my self-destructive behavior. I was also starting to understand that the source of the deep pain in my heart was the sin in my life, that there were consequences from my decisions, and those decisions separated me from having a personal relationship with my Lord and Savior, Jesus Christ!

I WAS SO EXCITED!

9TH INNING: THE GREATEST DECISION I HAVE EVER MADE

On Sunday July 21, 1996, I woke up and got ready for church. I was very excited that God was revealing to me that He loved me and wanted a personal relationship with me, if I would only trust Him. I was also nervous about giving my life to something other than baseball, since that was my identity for so long.

My mom asked what I was doing moving around the house like it was on fire. I asked her to hurry up and get dressed because I was going to get saved today! All those years she prayed for my salvation had paid off. She was going to see her son accept Jesus Christ today. Romans 10:13 says, *"Everyone who calls on the name of the Lord will be saved."*

How Do I Get Out?

When we got to church, I only remember one of the hymns we sang: "He Lives!" I don't remember the pastor's sermon or from where in the Bible he preached. I just remember thinking, *How am I going to get out of this row to get up front?* My mom and I were sitting in the middle of the row, and there were at least four people to our left and four people to our right. *How am I going to get out and get saved?*

I felt like a little child sitting in the car on the way to Disneyland asking, "Are we there yet? Are we there yet?" I was worried about missing the altar call.

I may not remember what the pastor preached, but I do remember when he invited me to receive Jesus Christ! Pastor Bill walked down the steps from the platform to the front of the auditorium. He asked, "Why are you coming forward?"

I said, "I want to get saved! I know in my heart that God is drawing me to Himself, and I want to give my life and heart to Jesus Christ."

He said, "If God is calling you to be saved, then I invite you to give your life and heart to Jesus Christ. If you want to know Jesus, then I will take you to Jesus."

Only a few minutes earlier, I was worried about how I was going to get out of that row to get to the front. But you know, I didn't need to worry about it because I got out of the row without a problem. And as I was walking down the aisle toward Pastor Bill, I glanced back at my mom; she was beaming with joy, like a very proud momma! She had tears running down her face.

Receiving a Free Gift

Pastor Bill asked me why I wanted to get saved. I said, "I am a sinner and I need a Savior; I believe that Jesus died on the cross for me. I believe He was crucified for me. I believe that His blood covers all my sins. I repent and come to Him by faith in the Son of God. I ask God to forgive me of all my sins, and I ask for God's love right now."

I asked God to save me in the name of Jesus Christ, Who is my Lord and Savior. And I thank God for saving me. Romans 10:9 says, *If you declare with your mouth, "Jesus is Lord," and believe in your heart that God raised him from the dead, you will be saved.*

Pastor Bill shared with the church that I just gave my life and heart to Jesus, and the church clapped and shouted a hearty praise and amen! I was given the free gift of salvation and a second-chance identity on July 21, 1996.

Sadly, I was not a Christian baseball player playing baseball for the glory of God. I was lost and separated from God, and that caused me a lot of pain and sorrow. I was always looking for acceptance.

The difference is now I have a relationship with God, and when the pain and sorrow comes, I can give them to God. I am playing (living) for a new manager! Matthew 11:28 says, *"Come to me, all you who are weary and burdened, and I will give you rest."*

Set Free

The day I gave my life and heart to Jesus Christ, He saved me set me free! John 8:36 says, *So if the Son sets you free, you will be free indeed.*

I was set free from the self-destructive behavior; I was set free from the hurt and pain that the alcohol and drugs caused me; I was set free from the guilt of my sin and the shame that came from the disappointment and the consequences of my decisions. I was no longer separated from a Holy God. For twenty-six years, there was a gap between God and me, and I could not close it on my own. It took the love of God sending His Son, Jesus, to be crucified and die on a cross to be the bridge that would lead me to God. John 14:6 says, *Jesus answered, "I am the way and the truth and the life. No one comes to the Father except through me."*

Before I came to Jesus, I followed a myth that I thought was a truth, a selfish way of life that only led me to pain and sorrow. But when I read the truth of God's Word that Jesus is the way, the truth, and the life, and that no one comes to the Father in heaven except through Him, I knew for that I needed a personal relationship with Jesus.

New Identity

I am now a new creation created in Christ Jesus. Second Corinthians 5:17 says, *Therefore, if anyone is in Christ, the new creation has come: The old has gone, the new is here!*

I was born again. I was clean from the inside out. The Bible says that the new creation has come—the old me is gone, and the new is here! I was brand-new, and that is exactly how I felt when I surrendered to the Lordship of Jesus Christ.

For the first time, I did not feel like I needed anyone's acceptance or approval. I did not have a desire to please man; I had a desire to please God.

I Want to Shout It!

I wanted to shout and tell the whole world about my new relationship with the Lord Jesus Christ, which was very new to me. I was good at living and shouting selfishly—for the me, myself, and I—but now I wanted to shout because God just saved me, forgave me, and redeemed me with His everlasting love. I was starting over with a second-chance identity. I wanted everyone to hear about my new relationship with Jesus and for all to know God personally—to have what I now had. I experienced God's love, God's grace, and God's mercy for the very first time, and it was exciting!

For twenty-six years, my identity was as a baseball player. I lived my life selfishly and pridefully, but now my identity was with Jesus Christ!

Now I live my life to please Him in everything I do. I live for His glory and praise.

A New Identity Declaration

God gave me—and He will give you—a new identity. Together we will live in the name of Jesus! Will you join me in living your life for Jesus Christ?

Will you declare with me that we will have nothing to do with irreverent and silly (godless) myths, but that we will train ourselves in godliness? Training our bodies has a limited benefit, but godliness is beneficial in every way, since it holds promises for the present life and for the life to come.

I labor and strive for Jesus Christ. I put all of my hope in Jesus Who is the living God and the Savior for those who believe.

Train Yourself Daily

First Timothy 4:7–10 says, *Have nothing to do with godless myths and old wives' tales; rather, train yourself to be godly. For physical training is of some value, but godliness has value for all things, holding promise for both the present life and the life to come. This is a trustworthy saying that deserves full acceptance. That is why we labor and strive, because we have put our hope in the living God, who is the Savior of all people, and especially of those who believe.*

Rob and Jill's
engagement and
wedding, 1997

Rob's first time preaching, 1996

Rob, head baseball coach at Crichton College, with Robby Jr., 2000

Rob and Faith Anne, 2003

JESUS IS LIFE . . . THE REST IS JUST DETAILS.

Extra Innings: Who Are You Playing For?

Do you have a personal relationship with Jesus Christ? Only God and you truly know. John 3:16 says, *For God so loved the world that he gave his one and only Son, that whoever believes in him shall not perish but have eternal life.*

I pray that if Jesus Christ is not your Lord and Savior, you will surrender and give your life to Him right now.

I invite you to call out to God and:

- **Admit** that you are a sinner in need of a Savior.

- **Believe** in your heart that Jesus died for you on the cross and that He was raised to life for you. Believe that Jesus conquered death, hell, and the grave.

- **Confess** Jesus as your Lord and Savior and surrender your life to God by faith and repentance.

- **Decide** to follow Jesus every moment of every day.

If you are thinking, *I would love to talk to someone about what this means to me*, I would love to talk with you, so please send me an e-mail message at rob@teamglorysports.org or send me a message through www.teamglorysports.org contact info.

I encourage you to seek out a Christian friend or a local pastor. I look back on how God used many people on my journey to becoming a Christian. They were there for me to talk with and spend time asking many questions about God's love and plan for my life, and for that I am so thankful.

I Want You to Know

I want you to know that everything I share in this book is my personal testimony and what God has said in His Word. The Bible is the inspired and infallible perfect Word of the living God. I have shared with you what God has said to do and what God has done for us by giving us His Son, Jesus Christ.

Extra Innings: I Love Living for Jesus

John 4:34–36 says, *"My food,"* said Jesus, *"is to do the will of him who sent me and to finish his work. Don't you have a saying, 'It's still four months until harvest'? I tell you, open your eyes and look at the fields! They are ripe for harvest. Even now the one who reaps draws a wage and harvests a crop for eternal life, so that the sower and the reaper may be glad together."*

For me, living for Jesus is about doing the will of God by serving Him wherever He sends me to go. I will continue serving Him until He calls me home or comes back to get me. God has called me to preach His gospel through a baseball and sports ministry and serve as a pastor. God has given me opportunities to coach and instruct baseball players in different areas of the United States and internationally. He has used my love of baseball to serve coaches and athletes by inspiring me to share the love of God through sports.

CPSIA information can be obtained
at www.ICGtesting.com
Printed in the USA
BVHW071222180921
617022BV00001B/31

9 781613 142837